HAMMOND

the dinosaur atlas

Mapmakers for the 21st Century

Published in the United States, Canada, and Puerto Rico
by Hammond World Atlas Corporation
Union, New Jersey 07083
www.hammondmap.com

Copyright © 2004 Orpheus Books Ltd.

Created and produced by Nicholas Harris, Claire Aston
and Emma Godfrey, Orpheus Books Ltd.

Text Steve Parker

Consultant Professor Michael Benton, Department of
Earth Sciences, Bristol University

Illustrated by Peter David Scott *(Wildlife Art Agency)* and
Gary Hincks

Other illustrators Peter Dennis, Inklink Firenze, Steve Kirk,
Nicki Palin, David Wright

ISBN 0-8437-1911-7

Printed and bound in Belgium.

CONTENTS

CRETACEOUS PERIOD

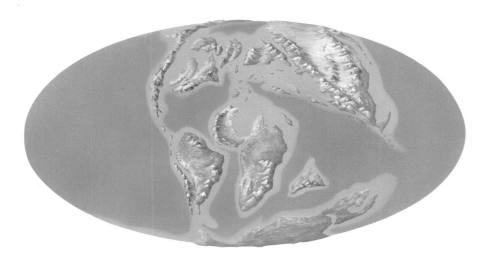

3

INTRODUCING THE DINOSAURS

Lizard (Komodo dragon)

DINOSAURS are some of the world's most famous animals. But no one has ever seen a real, living dinosaur because they all died out long ago. We know about these amazing beasts from their fossils. These are the hard body parts like bones, teeth, and claws, that were buried, trapped in rocks and turned to stone. Fossils show that dinosaurs were scaly reptiles, like today's crocodiles, lizards, snakes, and turtles. They spread across the world and ruled the land for 150 million years. Then, 65 million years ago, they all suddenly died out.

Dinosaurs stood and walked on straight legs, which were directly beneath their bodies. No other reptiles had straight, upright legs like this. Most reptiles, including today's lizards and tortoises, have legs at the sides of the body. They bend down at the knees. Prehistoric reptiles called thecodonts had partly bent legs, "halfway" between an ordinary reptile and a dinosaur. Thecodonts lived before the dinosaurs. Perhaps some of them changed, or evolved, into the first dinosaurs. Crocodiles can also walk in a partly-upright way.

Thecodont

Dinosaur

There were dinosaurs of almost every size, from tiny hunters no larger than a pet cat, to giants that were the biggest creatures ever to set foot on Earth. As far as we know, all dinosaurs had four limbs and a tail—unless bitten off by a predator. Some walked and ran on their two back legs. Others plodded along on all four. A few could do both. Most dinosaurs also had long necks and plenty of teeth.

But there is one feature we cannot know—a dinosaur's color. All of their fossils are turned to stone. Even rare finds of fossil dinosaur skin and scales are the color of rock. So, in pictures, their colors and patterns are guesses. Perhaps some dinosaurs were dull green or brown, like crocodiles, while others were bright colors, like lizards and snakes.

ORNITHISCHIANS

In an ornithischian dinosaur the two lower parts of the hip bone, known as the pubis and ischium, both slope down and back. They lie parallel with each other.

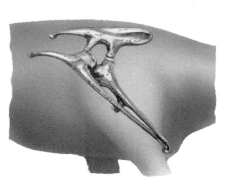

Dinosaurs were divided into two great groups according to the shape of their hip bone, or pelvis. They are the Saurischia or "lizard-hipped" dinosaurs and the Ornithischia or "bird-hipped" dinosaurs. Saurischians included all the meat-eaters, big and small, and the massive, long-necked, long-tailed, plant-eating sauropods like *Diplodocus* (DIP-low-DOE-cus). Ornithischians included all of the other dinosaurs, which as far as we know, all ate plants.

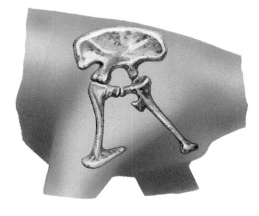

In a saurischian dinosaur the pubis slopes down and forward. It forms an upside-down V shape with the lower rear part, the ischium. (The third, upper part is the ilium.)

Like most reptiles today, and all birds, female dinosaurs laid eggs. Fossils have been found of many kinds of dinosaur eggs, and the nests where they were laid. There are also fossils of baby dinosaurs, just hatched from their eggs, and even some still inside their eggshells. These finds show that parent dinosaurs made nests for their eggs, and some stayed to guard their youngsters. Today, crocodiles and alligators are the only reptiles to do this. But it is not known if both dinosaur parents looked after the eggs and babies, or just the mother.

This illustration shows dinosaurs that lived in many parts of the world at different times. They are all drawn to scale. Many of the ornithischians have plates, horns, armor, or spikes, probably for defensive purposes. The saurischians, include both the theropods (meat-eaters), built for speed and power, and the long-necked, plant-eating sauropods.

Theropods　　　**S A U R I S C H I A N S**　　　**Sauropods**

THE COMING OF THE DINOSAURS

THE DINOSAURS were not the first animals on Earth. They first appeared about 230 million years ago, but life began more than 3,000 million years ago. Different kinds of plants and animals have evolved and died out. This huge amount of time is divided into periods (right). The dinosaurs lived during the Triassic, Jurassic, and Cretaceous periods.

During all of this time, Earth itself has changed too. Mountains have grown up and worn down. Seas and oceans flooded the land, then disappeared. Even the great landmasses, called continents, have moved—very slowly—around the globe.

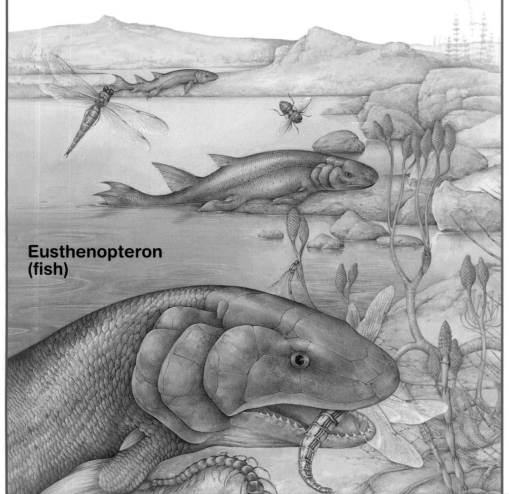

Eusthenopteron (fish)

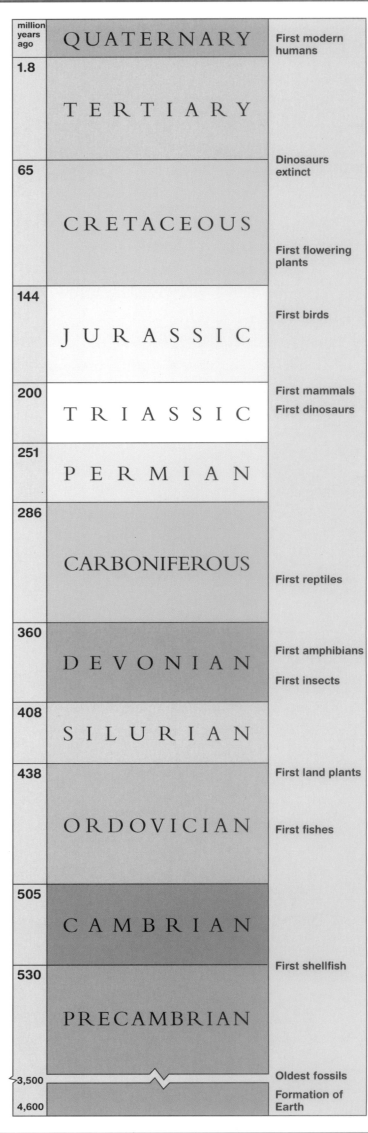

million years ago		
	QUATERNARY	First modern humans
1.8	TERTIARY	
65	CRETACEOUS	Dinosaurs extinct
		First flowering plants
144	JURASSIC	First birds
200	TRIASSIC	First mammals / First dinosaurs
251	PERMIAN	
286	CARBONIFEROUS	First reptiles
360	DEVONIAN	First amphibians / First insects
408	SILURIAN	
438	ORDOVICIAN	First land plants / First fishes
505	CAMBRIAN	First shellfish
530	PRECAMBRIAN	
3,500		Oldest fossils
4,600		Formation of Earth

Triassic

Jurassic

Hylonomus (early reptile)

Eryops (amphibian)

These three maps show what the world looked like through the Age of Dinosaurs, and how it changed. At first, in the Triassic Period, all of the main continents were joined together as one vast mass of land, known as Pangaea. During the Jurassic Period, the continents began to move apart. This drift continued through the Cretaceous Period. Sometimes sea levels rose and flooded land, then they fell to leave it dry again. So the shapes of the continents changed too.

Cretaceous

At first, there was life only in the ocean. The early plants and animals, such as seaweeds and jellyfish, were small and simple. Fish appeared about 500 million years ago. Then a few plants around the water's edge managed to survive in the air, and spread onto the land. Small animals followed them, such as ancient types of millipedes and insects.

By 370 million years ago the first four-legged animals, amphibians, waddled on to the land. Their limbs had evolved from the strong fins of certain fish *(opposite)*. But amphibians had to keep their skin moist, and go back to water to lay their eggs (as frogs and toads still do today). About 300 million years ago, another new group of creatures appeared. They had scaly skin and laid tough-shelled eggs. They could live on land all the time. They were the reptiles.

By the time of the Permian Period, just before the dinosaurs, reptiles had spread around the world. There were many shapes and sizes. *Dimetrodon* (die-MEET-row-don) was a fierce hunter 10 ft long. It had a tall flap of skin on its back, held up by bony rods. It was a type of reptile called a pelycosaur.

Dimetrodon

7

TRIASSIC WORLD

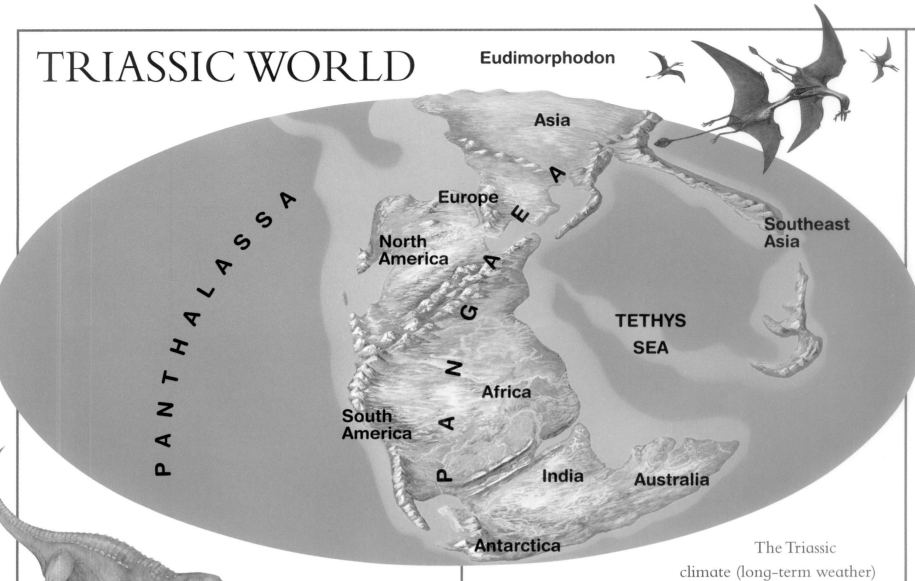

Eudimorphodon

Asia

Europe

North America

Southeast Asia

PANTHALASSA

PANGAEA

TETHYS SEA

Africa

South America

India

Australia

Antarctica

Euparkeria

THE AGE of Dinosaurs began with the Triassic Period, 251–200 million years ago. At this stage all lands of Earth were joined together as the vast supercontinent of Pangaea. Around it there was a large ocean, called Panthalassa.

As the waters rose and fell, they changed the outlines of the coast. So the continents looked different from their shapes on our modern maps. India was far away from the south of Asia, where it lies today. In Triassic times, it was located between Africa and Antarctica.

The Triassic climate (long-term weather) was warm and dry nearly everywhere. Many places were sandy or rocky, with tough plants. Into this world came the first dinosaurs. Perhaps they evolved from small reptiles like *Euparkeria* (YOU-park-EER-ee-ah). In South America almost 230 million years ago, the dinosaur *Herrerasaurus* (hair-AIR-ah-SORE-us) was a fast, sharp-toothed, 10-foot predator. *Riojasaurus* (REE-owe-jah-SORE-us) was a one-ton plant-eater.

Riojasaurus

Herrerasaurus

Mussaurus

Dinosaurs lived in Europe in the Late Triassic Period, 220 million years ago. One of the largest was *Plateosaurus* (plat-EE-owe-SORE-us), measuring 26 ft from nose to tail. *Plateosaurus* was a long-necked herbivore (plant-eater), peaceful unless attacked by the fearsome *Ornithosuchus* (or-NITH-owe-SOOK-us). This creature was not a dinosaur, but from another prehistoric reptile group called the thecodonts *(see page 4)*. *Saltopus*, just 2 ft long, was too tiny to worry *Plateosaurus*. But it was still a hungry hunter of insects and worms. Flying reptiles called pterosaurs, such as *Eudimorphodon (opposite)*, first appeared during the Triassic Period.

Plateosaurus

Ornithosuchus

Saltopus

North America was already busy with dinosaurs 225 million years ago. At 10 ft long, *Coelophysis* (SEEL-owe-FIE-sis) would have stood waist-high to a person. It was very slim and a fast runner on its strong back legs. Fossils of hundreds of these dinosaurs were found at a place called Ghost Ranch, in New Mexico. They were probably part of a large herd that died together in a sudden flood.

Coelophysis

DID YOU KNOW?

In the past few years, dinosaur fossils have been found in Madagascar, a large island to the east of Africa. They are as old as the fossils of early dinosaurs from South America. It seems that even by 228 million years ago, dinosaurs were already taking over!

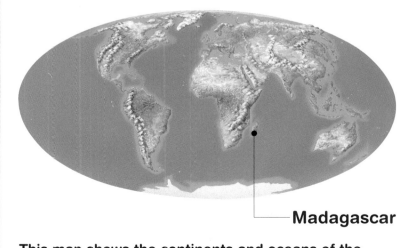

Madagascar

This map shows the continents and oceans of the world as they are positioned today.

JURASSIC WORLD

Asia

L A U R A S I A

P A N T H A L A S S A

North America

Europe

Southeast Asia

TETHYS SEA

Africa

India

G O N D W A N A

South America

Australia

Antarctica

Utahraptor

Pterodactylus

DURING the Jurassic Period, 200–144 million years ago, the vast land mass of Pangaea began to break up. The northern lands were called Laurasia. Across and around the Tethys Sea to the south was Gondwana. As the continents changed position, so did the climate, turning warmer and wetter in most parts.

A new group of meat-eating dinosaurs evolved in North America during the Jurassic. They were the "raptors," such as the 10-foot *Utahraptor* (YOU-tar-RAP-tore). They had a huge curved claw on each foot, to slash their victims. New pterosaurs flying in the Jurassic skies included *Pterodactylus* (TAIR-oh-DAK-tee-lus) from Europe.

With much more vegetation to eat, some kinds of dinosaur grew to enormous sizes.

Some of the biggest Jurassic dinosaurs lived in Africa. One was *Brachiosaurus* (BRACK-ee-owe-SORE-us). About 80 ft long, it was heavier than 10 elephants. And it was so tall, with its long front legs and towering neck, that it could have looked over a five-story building! *Brachiosaurus* had small, chisel-shaped teeth to chop leaves off conifer trees and the lower, pineapple-shaped trees called cycads. A much smaller African dinosaur, but very difficult to attack, was *Kentrosaurus* (KEN-troh-SORE-us). Strong bony plates stuck up from its back, and bony points from its tail. With sharp spikes at its tip, this dinosaur's tail was a dangerous weapon. *Kentrosaurus* was about the size and weight of a large family car. It belonged to the group called plated dinosaurs, or stegosaurs. Like *Brachiosaurus* it was a plant-eater, but it could only reach plants growing very near the ground.

Brachiosaurus

Kentrosaurus

One of the longest dinosaurs, at 90 ft, was *Diplodocus* (DIP-low-DOE-cus). Like *Brachiosaurus (above)*, it was a member of the dinosaur group called sauropods, and it lived in North America near the end of the Jurassic Period. It may have used its tail to whip at its enemies. Its teeth were like blunt pegs and hardly larger than your fingers. *Diplodocus* probably used them like a comb or rake. It pulled leaves off twigs and branches and swallowed them whole.

DID YOU KNOW?

Some dinosaurs ate stones. Massive plant-eaters like *Diplodocus* had no chewing teeth and swallowed food whole, along with small pebbles. These helped to mash the food in the dinosaur's huge, strong stomach. The smoothed pebbles are found with dinosaur fossils.

Diplodocus

This map shows the continents and oceans of the world as they are positioned today.

JURASSIC PERIOD

NORTH AMERICA

DURING the Jurassic Period, North America lay very close to Europe. The Atlantic Ocean, which now separates them, had not yet opened up. There was no link to South America, as there is today, across Central America. The polar regions—what is now Alaska and Canada—had no ice or snow, even in winter. The climate was far too warm. Forests covered vast areas of North America. The main trees were conifers like redwoods and Chile pine. Ginkgo or maidenhair trees were also plentiful. They provided a great deal of food for the huge Jurassic dinosaurs.

A large killer of the early Jurassic was *Dilophosaurus* (DIE-low-fow-SORE-us). It had two curved ridges of bone on its head.

ASIA

Aleutian Islands

PACIFIC OCEAN

Dilophosaurus

Seismosaurus

North America had many kinds of giant sauropod dinosaurs. They had tiny heads, long necks and tails, barrel-shaped bodies and elephant-like legs. To nourish their great bulk, they spent all day eating leaves. Only a few fossils of *Seismosaurus* (SIZE-mow-SORE-us) have ever been found. But if it was similar in shape to other wellknown sauropods like *Diplodocus*, then *Seismosaurus* would have been even longer—perhaps 130 ft, or almost the width of a football field. The name *Seismosaurus* means "earth-shaking lizard." The ground certainly shook as this beast thundered along!

With so much warmth and rain, many parts of North America were covered by muddy swamps and marshes. *Diplodocus*, and the shorter but heavier *Apatosaurus* (a-PAT-owe-SORE-us), stripped leaves from tall trees.

Stegosaurus (STEG-owe-SORE-us) had tall plates of bone on its humped back. Perhaps these soaked up the sun's heat, so that *Stegosaurus* could be warmer and more active. It swished its spiky tail to defend its young against the fierce two-horned predator *Ceratosaurus* (sair-RAT-owe-SORE-us).

Apatosaurus

Greenland

EUROPE

RTH

RICA

AFRICA

**SOUTH
AMERICA**

Allosaurus

Camarasaurus

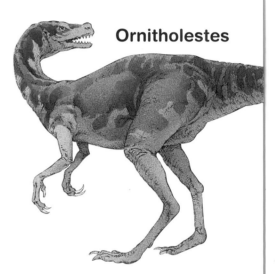

Ornitholestes

The terror of the late Jurassic, 150 million years ago, was *Allosaurus* (AL-low-SORE-us). This massive meat-eater was 35 ft long and weighed about 2 tons. Its teeth were bigger than your hands, and it could run faster than a champion human sprinter. *Allosaurus* chased after big prey, like the 20-ton sauropod dinosaur *Camarasaurus* (CAM-are-ah-SORE-us). Smaller meat-eaters such as *Ornitholestes* (or-NITH-owe-LEST-eez) picked over the remains, or hunted their own victims such as lizards, frogs, and insects.

Diplodocus

Ceratosaurus

Stegosaurus

DID YOU KNOW?

More huge kinds of dinosaurs are known from North America during the Jurassic, than from any other continent during any other time period.

This map shows North America (colored red) as it is today.

JURASSIC PERIOD

13

EUROPE

Dimorphodon

THE CONTINENT of Europe, in the Jurassic Period, was very different from the Europe of today. Much of what is now dry land was covered by shallow seas, lagoons, freshwater lakes, and marshes. Only a few areas, such as present-day France and Spain, were above the surface. The conditions did not suit many dinosaurs. But the warm, shallow waters were very suitable for preserving all kinds of animals as fossils. As their dead bodies rotted along shores and in the water, their bones and other hard parts sank to the sea bed. Covered by sand, mud, or silt, they gradually turned to stone.

Rhamphorhynchus

Greenland

NORTH AMERICA

Scotland

NORTHERN

France

Spain

SOUTHERN

AFRICA

Scelidosaurus (skell-ID-owe-SORE-us) was about the same size as an average crocodile of today. Its fossils date back to early Jurassic times, 200 million years ago. They have been found in England, as well as North America, and East Asia. *Scelidosaurus* was an armored dinosaur. It had bony lumps, called scutes, all over its body. Spiky scutes ran along its back and tail, while cone-shaped scutes were found on its sides. This body armor protected *Scelidosaurus* against meat-eaters. In the skies above flew pterosaurs such as *Dimorphodon* (die-MORF-owe-don) and, later in the Jurassic, *Rhamphorhynchus* (RAM-foh-RINK-us).

By the Late Jurassic Period, 155-150 million years ago, many sizes and kinds of dinosaurs roamed Europe.

Scelidosaurus

Small meat-eating dinosaur

Feathered dinosaur

Archaeopteryx

Scandinavia

E U R O P E

Germany

ASIA

E U R O P E

T E T H Y S S E A

India

Compsognathus

One of the earliest known birds was *Archaeopteryx* (ARK-ee-OP-tair-icks). Its fossils come from Late Jurassic rocks in southern Germany. The amazing details on these fossils show the tooth-filled beak and the long bony tail of *Archaeopteryx*, and even its delicate feathers. Most experts believe that birds evolved from small dinosaurs. The skeleton of the swift, meat-eating dinosaur *Compsognathus* (komp-sog-NAY-thus), just 3 ft long, was very similar to that of *Archaeopteryx*. *Compsognathus* also lived in southern Germany and at the same time, 150 million years ago.

Archaeopteryx

The enormous meat-eater *Megalosaurus* (MEG-ah-low-SORE-us) hunted the even larger plant-eater *Cetiosaurus* (SET-ee-owe-SORE-us), 50 ft in length. Another herbivore, less than 3 ft long, was *Echinodon* (ee-KINE-owe-don).

DID YOU KNOW?
Megalosaurus was one of the first three dinosaurs to be given a scientific name, about 180 years ago. *Iguanodon* and *Hylaeosaurus* were the others.

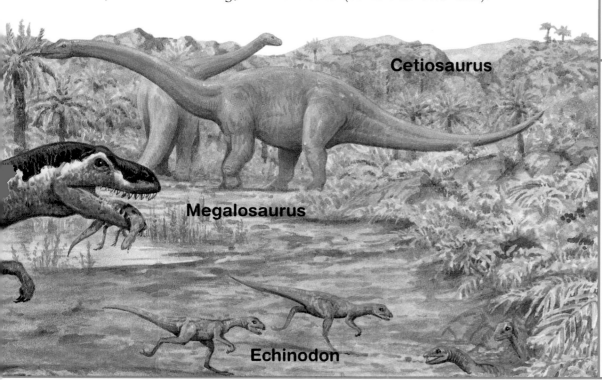

Cetiosaurus

Megalosaurus

Echinodon

This map shows Europe (colored red) as it is today.

JURASSIC PERIOD

ASIA

THE GREAT continent of Asia teemed with Jurassic dinosaurs. Asia was then not quite as vast as it is today. The high sea levels of the time flooded some of the land. India was missing. It was still far away, close to Africa. It would take millions of years to drift slowly north and join with Asia. Europe and Asia meet at the Ural Mountains today, but in Jurassic times they were separated by a narrow strait.

Euhelopus (YOU-hell-OWE-pus) was a Late Jurassic sauropod from China.

Euhelopus

EUROPE

Ural Mountains

A S

West Asia

Future

AFRICA

Pterosaurs spread to Asia in the Jurassic Period.

A fierce and powerful predator from China, *Yangchuanosaurus* (yang-CHWAN-owe-SORE-us) was 30 ft long. It may have hunted the massive sauropod *Euhelopus (above).*

Yangchuanosaurus

In the middle of the Jurassic Period, dinosaurs thrived in East Asia. Giants included *Mamenchisaurus* and another sauropod, *Shunosaurus* (SHOO-no-SORE-us), which had a spiky tail club to swing at its enemies. *Tuojiangosaurus* (toh-HWAN-go-SORE-us) was a type of stegosaur about 20 ft long. The spikes on its back and tail defended it against the deadly meat-eater, *Yangchuanosaurus (left).* Tiny *Xiaosaurus* (SHEE-ah-oh-SORE-us) ran about in the undergrowth looking for ferns and other plants to eat.

Xiaosaurus

Huayangosaurus

Huayangosaurus (hoo-eye-YAN-go-SORE-us), 13 ft long, lived in Middle Jurassic times in China. It was an early type of stegosaur, with plates and spikes of bone running along its back and tail. Later the stegosaurs spread to other continents, especially North America.

Siberia

Japan

China

Himalayas

Southeast Asia

TETHYS SEA

Mamenchisaurus (ma-MEN-kee-SORE-us) was named for a stream in China, the Mamen, where its fossils were first discovered. At 80 ft long and 25 tons in weight, this sauropod was one of the biggest dinosaurs known. It lived 160 million years ago and had the longest neck, 50 ft, of any animal ever. At the end of the Jurassic Period, most sauropods died out. Only a few survived into the Cretaceous.

Mamenchisaurus

Mamenchisaurus

Shunosaurus

Tuojiangosaurus

Yangchuanosaurus

DID YOU KNOW?
During the past 25 years, more fossils of dinosaurs and other prehistoric animals have been found in China than anywhere else in the world.

This map shows Asia (colored red) as it is today.

JURASSIC PERIOD

CRETACEOUS WORLD

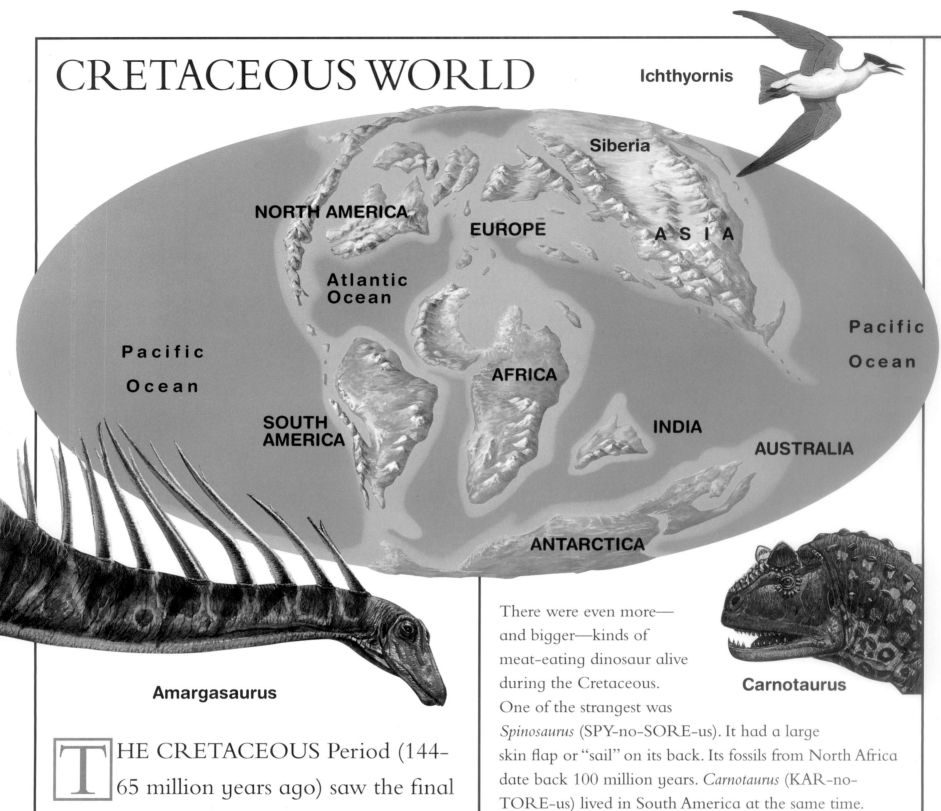

Ichthyornis

Siberia

NORTH AMERICA

EUROPE

A S I A

Atlantic Ocean

Pacific Ocean

Pacific Ocean

AFRICA

SOUTH AMERICA

INDIA

AUSTRALIA

ANTARCTICA

Amargasaurus

Carnotaurus

THE CRETACEOUS Period (144–65 million years ago) saw the final breakup of the great supercontinents, Laurasia and Gondwana. Vast, shallow seas covered much of North America and Europe. Chalk rocks formed on the beds of these seas, giving the Cretaceous Period its name (creta is an ancient word for "chalk"). There was a gradual change in the climate too. It became cooler and drier. There were also changing seasons around the world.

There were even more— and bigger—kinds of meat-eating dinosaur alive during the Cretaceous. One of the strangest was *Spinosaurus* (SPY-no-SORE-us). It had a large skin flap or "sail" on its back. Its fossils from North Africa date back 100 million years. *Carnotaurus* (KAR-no-TORE-us) lived in South America at the same time. Perhaps it tackled *Amargasaurus* (am-ARG-ah-SORE-us), an unusual, spiny-necked sauropod.

Spinosaurus

The hadrosaurs are called "duck-bills" because the front of the mouth was wide and flat, like a duck's beak. Some had shapes of hollow bone on their heads, perhaps to blow through and make noises, like *Corythosaurus* (KOH-rith-owe-SORE-us) and *Lambeosaurus* (LAM-bee-owe-SORE-us). *Edmontosaurus* (ed-MONT-owe-SORE-us) had a bag of skin on its nose, maybe for the same reason.

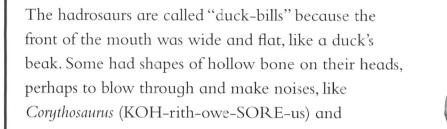

Corythosaurus

Edmontosaurus

Lambeosaurus

Minmi

DID YOU KNOW?

Hadrosaurs (duck-billed dinosaurs) had no teeth at the front of their beaklike mouths. But farther back in the mouth were long rows of ridged cheek teeth, for extra-powerful chewing. Some types of hadrosaurs had more than 1,000 teeth!

As the continents began to separate, each carried its own dinosaurs. Cut off from others of their kind, the groups began to evolve, to suit the changing conditions in their own region. That is why so many new and different kinds of dinosaurs appeared during the Cretaceous Period.

Minmi (MIN-mee) was an ankylosaur (armored dinosaur). But it was just 10 ft long—much smaller than other ankylosaurs. It is named for the place where its fossils were found, Minmi Crossing, in Australia. It snipped off leaves and plants to eat with its beak-shaped mouth, 115 million years ago.

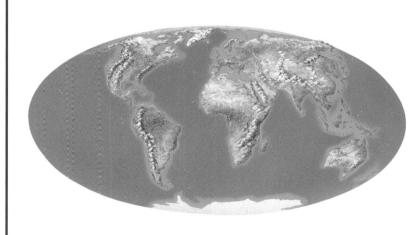

This map shows the continents and oceans of the world as they are located today.

NORTH AMERICA

BY THE CRETACEOUS Period, the continent of North America had drifted away from Europe and South America, although it was still connected to Asia. The climate was warmer than today and what is today the freezing Arctic Ocean was free of ice.

North America was divided into several large islands by warm, shallow seas. The Western Interior Seaway split the continent down the middle, and joined up with what is now Hudson Bay in the north and the Gulf of Mexico in the south.

On land, flowering plants and broadleaf trees spread among the coniferous forests that once covered North America.

Pteranodon

Quetzalcoatlus

PACIFIC OCEAN

N O

A M E

Western Interior Seaway

The Cretaceous skies were dominated by giant pterosaurs like *Pteranodon* and *Quetzalcoatlus (see page 27).*

Deinonychus

A fierce predator, *Deinonychus* (die-NON-ee-kus), whose name means "terrible claw," had powerful jaws lined with razor-sharp teeth, curved like daggers. But its most lethal weapon was a huge, scythe-like claw on each of its feet. It stood only about as tall as a 10-year-old, although its long, stiffened tail made it as long as a small car. Several *Deinonychus* hunting together could bring down much larger prey.

Triceratops (try-SERR-ah-tops) roamed through the forest in herds. Its head and neck were protected by a large frill of solid bone, while the three large horns on its head were good defense against attacks by flesh-eaters.

Triceratops

A duck-billed dinosaur, *Parasaurolophus* (PA-ra-sore-oh-LOAF-us), had a backward-pointing crest measuring up to 7 ft long. It was hollow, and may have turned its calls into loud, bellowing sounds. *Pachycephalosaurus* (PAK-ee-SEFF-a-loh-SORE-us) had a domed head. Made of thick, solid bone, it may have been used for head-butting by males.

ASIA

Greenland

EUROPE

AFRICA

SOUTH AMERICA

Parasaurolophus

Pachycephalo-saurus

Almost completely covered by thick, bony plates, *Euoplocephalus* (yoo-OP-low-SEFF-ah-lus) was very well protected. Spikes stuck out from its head and neck. It even had bony eye-lids. At the end of its tail was a huge ball of bone that acted like a club.

Euoplocephalus

Tyrannosaurus' (tie-RAN-oh-SORE-us) massive jaws had rows of saw-edged teeth, some up to 7 in long. It rushed at its victims, bringing them down with its teeth or feet. Its tiny arms might have pinned down its prey while its foot-claws did the rest.

Tyrannosaurus

DID YOU KNOW?
Nearly all of North America's long-necked sauropods died out in the Cretaceous. These plant-eaters were succeeded by duck-billed and horned dinosaurs.

This map shows North America (colored red) as it is today.

EUROPE

Ornithocheirus

ODAY, Europe has two main islands—Britain and Ireland. Back in Cretaceous times, Europe was almost all islands, surrounded by wide shallow seas. Only the hills and mountains of Scandinavia in the north towered above the waters. Nearly all southeastern Europe was under the waves. There was also a strait between Europe and Asia, where the Ural Mountains now stand. Many new kinds of dinosaurs evolved on these islands. Some were able to feast on the new flowering plants, such as herbs and blossom trees, which brought fresh colors to the landscape.

Criorhynchus

The pterosaurs of the Cretaceous Period no longer had the long, trailing tails of their Jurassic cousins, but short ones. *Criorhynchus* (KRY-oh-RIN-kus) had wings measuring more than 16 ft across.

Greenland

Scotland

England

France

ATLANTIC
OCEAN

Spain

NORTH AMERICA

NORTH

Hypsilophodon

Today's world has a wide variety of small plant-eating mammals such as rabbits and rats. The Cretaceous world was similar, except that the small herbivores were dinosaurs, such as *Hypsilophodon* (HIP-see-LOW-foe-don). It was only 7 ft long and would have stood waist-high to a person. Groups of *Hypsilophodon* probably ran quickly through the undergrowth, eating soft leaves and ferns. Its fossils were found in England and Spain.

Somewhere in what is now southern England, about 120 million years ago, lurked the fearsome predator *Baryonyx* (BARR-ee-on-ICKS). It was 30 ft long and 2 tons in weight. Its long, low head, with rows of small, sharp teeth, were suited to grabbing slippery prey such as fish. Perhaps it scooped these out of rivers and lakes, using the big, curved claws on its thumbs. In this scene, small *Hypsilophodon* scurry away from the meat-eater, while a herd of *Iguanodon* pull the leaves from trees with their beaklike mouths.

Scandinavia

A S I A

Germany

R O P E

WEST ASIA

Iguanodon

Acrocanthosaurus

INDIAN OCEAN

AFRICA

Iguanodon (ig-WAH-no-DON) was a large and powerful plant-eater, measuring about 30 ft long and weighing almost 5 tons. Thousands of its fossils have been found in many places across Europe, including England, Germany, and Spain. It had a long spike on each thumb, which it could jab into its enemies such as *Acrocanthosaurus* (ak-roe-CAN-thoe-SORE-us).

Iguanodon

Hypsilophodon

Baryonyx

DID YOU KNOW?

The Isle of Wight, off the coast of southern England, has so many fossil-filled rocks from the Cretaceous Period that it is called "Dinosaur Island."

This map shows Europe (colored red) as it is today.

CRETACEOUS PERIOD

ASIA

ACROSS the world during the Cretaceous Period, there was only about half as much dry land as there is today. The oceans were much greater. Most of the land was in the biggest continent, Asia. The south of Asia, where the massive Himalaya mountains now stand, was a chain of hilly islands and lagoons. Most dinosaur fossils from the Cretaceous Period in Asia have been found in the east, in Mongolia and China.

Sinornis

Dsungaripterus

During the Cretaceous, more birds flew in the skies, such as sparrow-sized *Sinornis* (Sin-OR-nis). Some pterosaurs were huge. *Dsungaripterus* (ZOON-gar-IP-tair-us) had a wingspan of more than 10 ft.

EUROPE

ASIA

Arabia

AFRICA

INDIA

Oviraptor

Oviraptor (OH-vee-RAP-tor) means "egg-stealer." When fossils of this dinosaur were found in Mongolia, they were among broken egg-shells. Experts thought *Oviraptor* had been eating dinosaur eggs or babies. It now seems that the eggs belonged to *Oviraptor* itself, and it died sitting on its nest. Even so, its powerful beaklike mouth was ideal for cracking open eggs!

Today, most of Mongolia is dry, cold, and windy. About 80 million years ago it was also fairly dry, but slightly warmer. Bushes and shrubs grew in the sandy soil. The tanklike, armored *Saichania* (sye-CHAN-ee-ah), 20 ft long, munched low plants. Protected by spikes and bony studs, *Saichania* was ready to hammer any predator that came too near with its club-ended tail. *Protoceratops* guarded its nest from the possible egg-thief *Oviraptor*. The fastest runner of the time was the beaked ostrich-dinosaur, *Gallimimus*.

Protoceratops

Velociraptor

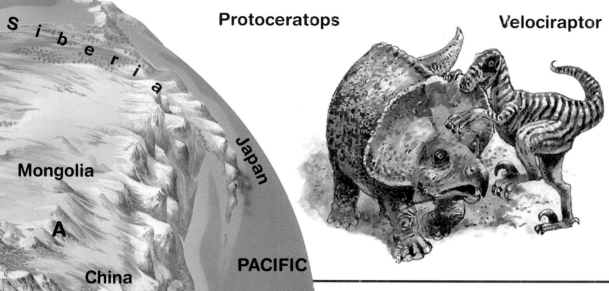

One amazing fossil find shows how two dinosaurs battled to the death about 80 million years ago in the sands of East Asia. *Protoceratops* (PROH-toe-SAIR-ah-tops) was a pig-sized cousin of *Triceratops (see page 20)*. It was attacked by a fierce hunter, *Velociraptor* (vel-OSS-ee-RAP-tore). *Protoceratops* bit with its powerful beak, *Velociraptor* slashed with its foot claws—and both died.

Some of the strangest dinosaurs were the "ostrich-dinosaurs" such as *Gallimimus* (GALL-ee-MEE-mus). They were very similar in size and shape to the ostrich of today, except that they had a long, bony tail, and scales rather than feathers. Ostrich-dinosaurs were built for speed. Their long, slim mouth was shaped just like a bird's beak. Most had no teeth at all. *Gallimimus* probably pecked for food such as leaves, roots, seeds, and small animals like insects, worms, and lizards.

Gallimimus

DID YOU KNOW?
During Cretaceous times in Asia, several kinds of dinosaurs had feathers! Their arms were too small to fly. Perhaps the feathers kept them warm.

This map shows Asia (colored red) as it is today.

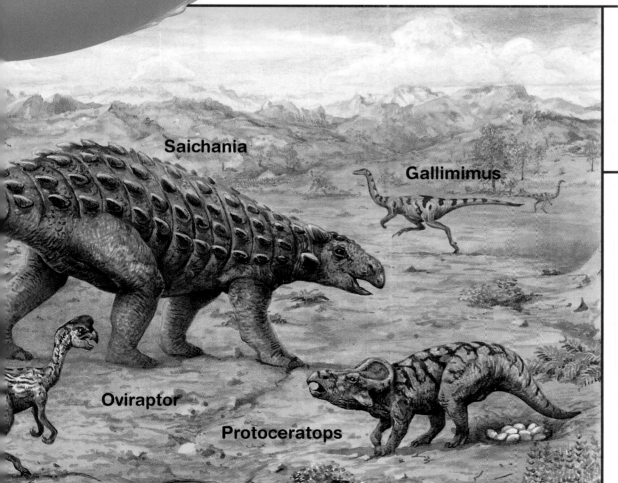

Siberia

Mongolia

China

Japan

PACIFIC OCEAN

Future Himalayas

Southeast Asia

INDIAN OCEAN

Saichania

Gallimimus

Oviraptor

Protoceratops

CRETACEOUS PERIOD

SEA REPTILES

DINOSAURS ruled the land, but they did not rule the seas. No dinosaurs lived in the water all the time. But many other kinds of reptiles did. From the Triassic Period and on through the Age of Dinosaurs, various groups of big, fierce reptiles swam in the oceans. Most were hunters, chasing prey such as fish, squid, and shellfish.

In many ways, the marine (sea-dwelling) reptiles were similar to dinosaurs. They had scaly skin, big eyes for seeing well, plenty of teeth, four limbs, and a tail. But their limbs were not legs for running—they were paddles or flippers for swimming. Like both the dinosaurs on land and pterosaurs in the air, the sea reptiles breathed air. They could not breathe underwater, like fish. So they had to stay near the surface, and poke their heads out now and again for fresh air, before diving below the waves.

Nothosaurus

Placodus

Ichthyosaurus (ICK-thee-owe-SORE-us) was one of the fastest swimmers. It had a smooth, sleek shape and a big tail, which it swished from side to side to power through the water. Different kinds of ichthyosaurs lived through the Jurassic Period and into the Cretaceous. Some were 50 ft long.

Macroplata (plesiosaur)

Eurhinosaurus (ichthyosaur)

Teleosaurus (crocodile)

The first big sea reptiles, in the Triassic, were placodonts and nothosaurs *(left)*. *Nothosaurus* (NO-thoe-SORE-us) was 10 ft long. Its fossils occur in ancient sea-bed rocks now on three continents—Europe, Asia, and Africa. It probably dived to catch food, then waddled with its webbed feet on to the shore to rest.

Placodus (plack-OWE-dus) was slightly smaller, 7 ft long. It was not such a good swimmer. Perhaps it searched for shellfish along the beach and at the water's edge, crushing them with its large, flat teeth.

Ichthyosaurus

Like some dinosaurs, some sea reptiles became enormous. *Elasmosaurus* (ee-LAZ-mow-SORE-us) was 50 ft—longer than *Tyrannosaurus* on land. But most of it consisted of an amazingly long, thin neck. Perhaps *Elasmosaurus* paddled at the surface, head high above. When it spotted prey, it darted its head in, to grab the victim with its long, sharp teeth.

Animals at the sea's surface were in danger from other predators. Pterosaurs swooped down, flapping their huge wings, ready to snatch a meal in their long beaks. *Pteranodon* (tair-AN-oh-DON) had a strange point on the back of its head, like a witch's hat. *Quetzalcoatlus* (KET-zahl-koe-AT-lus) was the largest flying animal that ever lived, with wings up to 40 ft across!

Pteranodon

Plesiosaurus (plesiosaur)

Quetzalcoatlus

Elasmosaurus

Ichthyosaur

By the Jurassic, the oceans teemed with big reptiles *(above)*. Plesiosaurs had a large body with a flipper at each corner, a long neck, and sharp teeth. Ichthyosaurs looked quite like dolphins. Many had a long, pointed snout. One group of Jurassic reptiles survives today, but mainly in fresh water—crocodiles.

EXTINCTION OF THE DINOSAURS

FOR MORE than 160 million years, hundreds of different kinds of dinosaurs evolved. They lived and died, some leaving behind their fossils in the rocks. Then, quite suddenly, about 65 million years ago, they were gone. There are no more fossils of dinosaurs after this time, which was the end of the Cretaceous Period.

Not only the dinosaurs died out. Sea reptiles, such as ichthyosaurs and plesiosaurs, also disappeared. So did the pterosaurs, along with many kinds of shellfish in the oceans, and even huge numbers of plants. Three-quarters of life on Earth vanished for ever. The sudden death of so many living things is called a mass extinction. What caused this terrible disaster and killed off the dinosaurs?

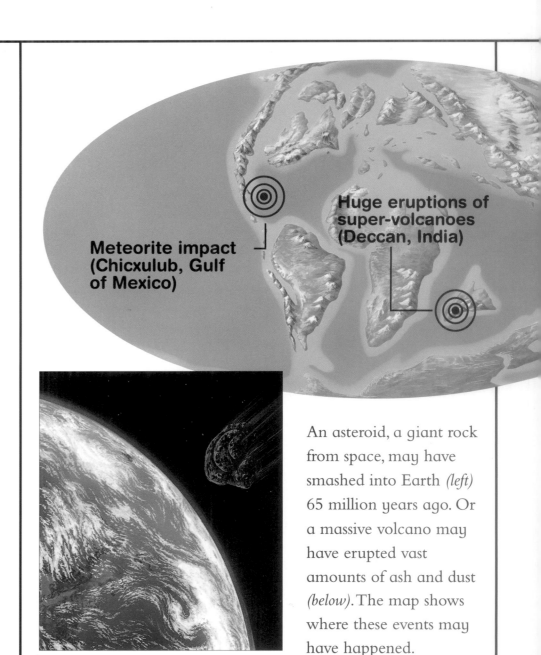

Meteorite impact (Chicxulub, Gulf of Mexico)

Huge eruptions of super-volcanoes (Deccan, India)

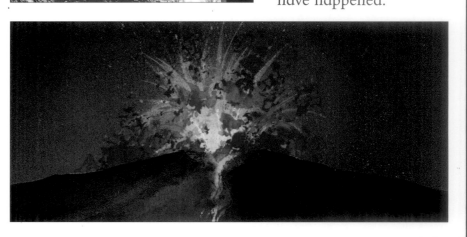

An asteroid, a giant rock from space, may have smashed into Earth *(left)* 65 million years ago. Or a massive volcano may have erupted vast amounts of ash and dust *(below)*. The map shows where these events may have happened.

If a giant asteroid had hit Earth, it would have thrown up clouds of dust to blot out the sun. Volcano ash and dust could have done the same. A very long winter began. Plants withered away. Dinosaurs perished from cold and hunger.

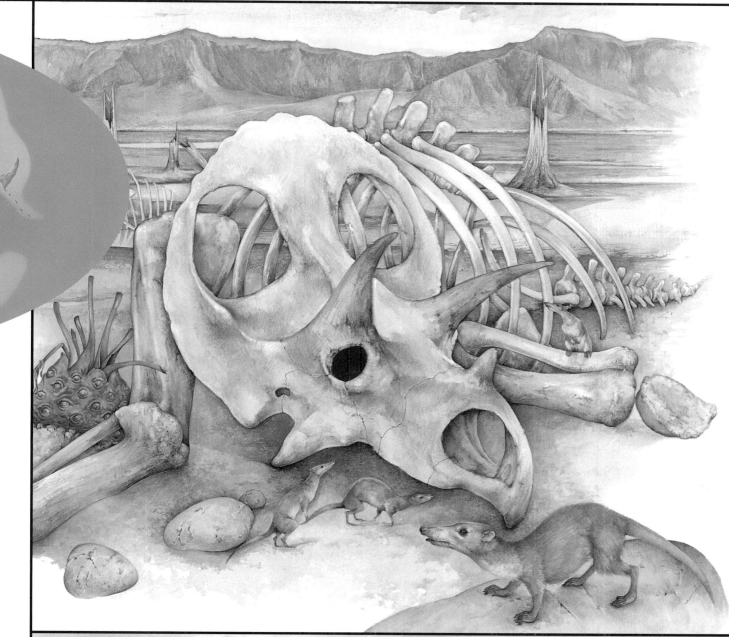

The end of the Cretaceous Period, 65 million years ago, was the end of the Age of Dinosaurs. Those great reptiles which had ruled the world for so long became piles of bones across the land.

But some animals survived. For almost all of the Age of Dinosaurs, small, furry creatures lived in the shadows, daring to come out to feed only at night. They were mammals. With dinosaurs gone, their time had come. Very soon, mammals and birds—both groups were warm-blooded—began to evolve into many different kinds the world over.

After the Cretaceous came the Tertiary Period, 65-1.8 million years ago. Continents carried on drifting, to where they lie today.

Life continued to evolve. Many new kinds of mammals and birds appeared. But, apart from the whales, they never reached the gigantic size of the dinosaurs.

REDISCOVERING THE DINOSAURS

OUR WORLD today seems full of dinosaurs. We see them in museums, theme parks, movies, books, and cartoons. But all of these dinosaurs, with their bright colors and terrifying roars, are guesswork.

All we really have left from the dinosaurs are their fossils. These are the hard body parts, like bones, teeth, claws, and horns, preserved in rocks. But fossils can tell us a great deal—as long as they are dug up with great care, and studied in great detail.

Fossil-hunting is easiest where rocks are not covered by soil, trees, and plants. The fossils can be seen at the surface, or dug out from just beneath. Many dinosaur fossil sites are in bare, rocky areas with hills and cliffs, far from roads or towns. They include the North American Midwest, Argentina, Europe, Southeast Africa, Mongolia, China, and Australia.

NORTH AMERICA

SOUTH AMERICA

ANTARCTICA

Through the ages, millions of fossils have formed—not only from dinosaurs, but all kinds of living things. The hard, tough body parts, such as shells (1), were most likely to be preserved. Most fossils formed in water as the hard remains were covered by sand or mud (2). As the layers piled up, the lower ones were pressed together and turned into solid rock, along with the body parts inside, which became fossils (3). After millions of years of earth movements and the wearing away of rocks by water, wind, and ice, some fossils returned to the surface (4).

Not only body parts formed fossils. Signs of animals did too, like footprints made in mud (*right*) or skin imprints. The depth of the prints and the distance between them, tell us how fast a dinosaur walked or ran.

The place where fossils are found is known as the "dig." Paleontologists, scientists who study fossils, carry out the painstaking work of getting the fossils out of the ground. Soil and loose lumps are removed with pick-axes and shovels. Tiny bits of rock are chipped away much more carefully using little hammers, chisels, and scrapers. Loose sand and dust are carefully brushed aside, often with toothbrushes.

At every stage, the rocks and fossils are measured, drawn, photographed, described in writing, then taken away. A tiny detail noticed at this stage can be important later. Some fossils and their lumps of rock might break up easily. To take them back to the workroom, they are covered with plaster casings—like a broken leg!

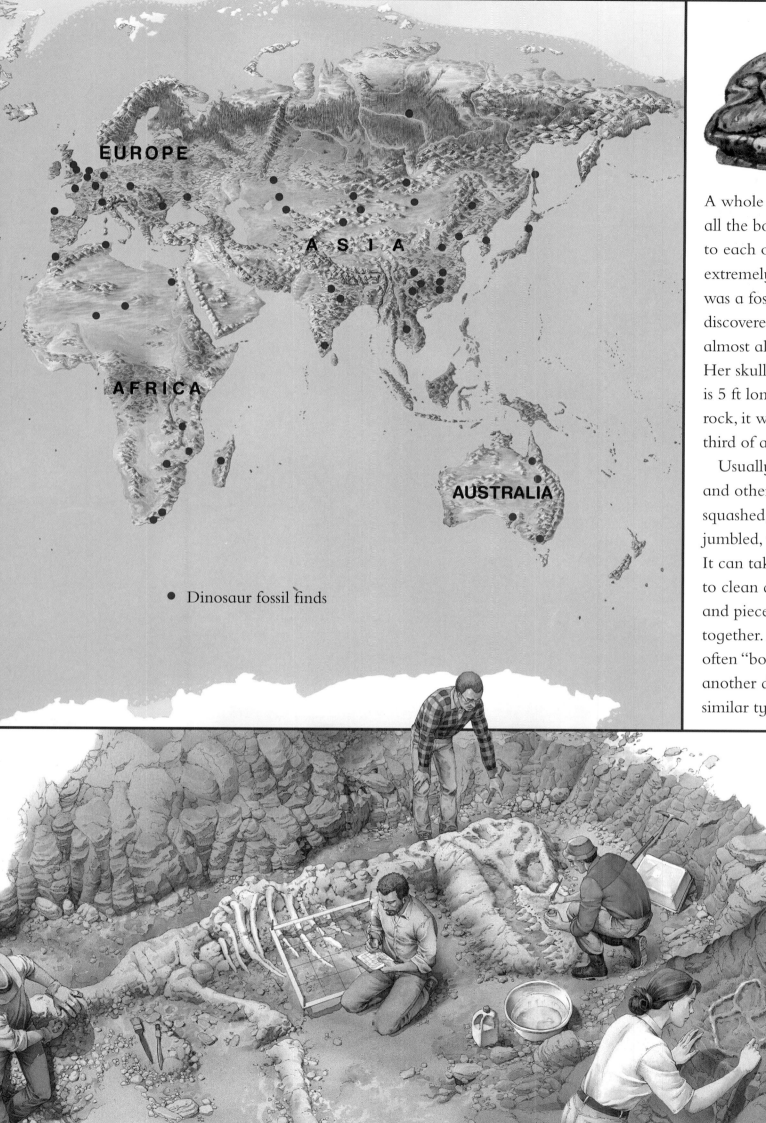

EUROPE

ASIA

AFRICA

AUSTRALIA

• Dinosaur fossil finds

A whole fossil dinosaur, with all the bones in place, next to each other, is an extremely rare find. "Sue" was a fossil *Tyrannosaurus* discovered in 1990, with almost all her parts present. Her skull, slightly squashed, is 5 ft long. Being of solid rock, it weighs about one-third of a ton.

Usually the bones, teeth, and other fossil parts are squashed, broken, and jumbled, with many missing. It can take months or years to clean all the rock away and piece the fossils together. Missing parts are often "borrowed" from another dinosaur of a similar type.

INDEX